COTSWOLD BORN N'BRED

MY LIFE AT SNOWSHILL
by Bob Hodge

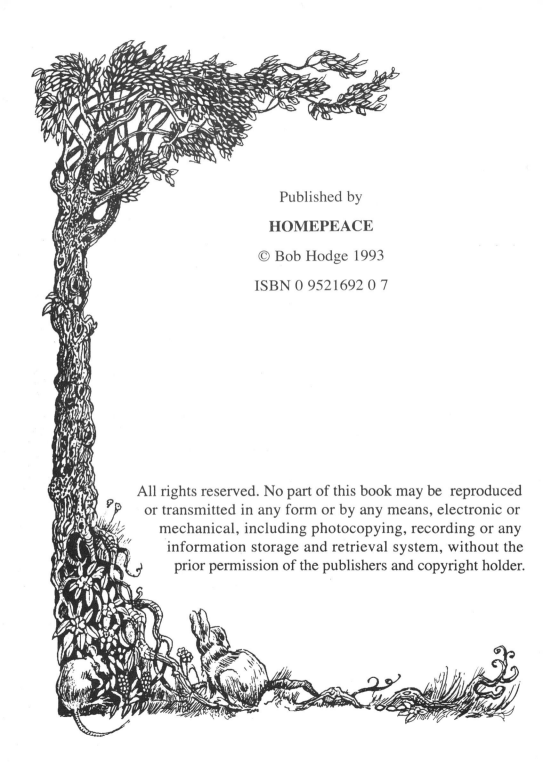

Published by

HOMEPEACE

© Bob Hodge 1993

ISBN 0 9521692 0 7

INTRODUCTION

A few years ago, I had a letter from the Snowshill Women's Club asking me if I would give a talk on my years at Snowshill. As I had never given a speech or talk in my life before, my answer was "sorry, I can remember quite a lot and could probably write it all down, but I would be hopeless in front of an audience." After a lot of persuasion, I agreed to think it over and let them know in a week.

That little conversation started my thoughts going back to my boyhood, and all the changes that had taken place in the many years I had lived at Snowshill.

So I started making notes, and it's surprising the number of things that came to mind. In the end I finished up with two pages of notes and after a couple of drinks, I plucked up courage and gave the talk. Surprisingly, when I got started things went quite well, and I rambled on for about an hour and a half and then only about half of my notes had been used. Everyone seemed interested and asked a lot of questions, which helped a lot.

Most of the women were new-comers to the village which made things much easier for me, so that if I made a few mistakes with the dates and so on, no one knew any different. Since that little talk and having a lot of spare time, I thought that I would try and write a kind of diary about all the things that have happened in my years at Snowshill. I began these notes in 1982 and completed them in 1990.

ACKNOWLEDGEMENTS

The author and his son would like to thank the following people for their help, encouragement and expertise in producing this little book:-

Curt, Alison and Mimi Garfield for their tremendous enthusiasm and practical help at all stages.

Jessica Hemming for initial type design, layout and ideas.

Jean Sidinius, who originally suggested publication.

Barbara Turner, Linda Roberts, 'The Evesham Journal' and 'The Richard Hagen Gallery' for the use of pictures and photographs.

Maureen Butler and Tony Buttler for proof reading

Alan, Ian, Steve, Dave and the printing staff at BBC Wood Norton for their help in producing the first edition.

With special thanks to Tim Harrison for planting the seed of an idea to reprint this book and to Dean Andrews for helping to bring it to fruition.

Reprinted and Bound in 2005 by:

Quorum Technical Services Ltd, Units 3 & 4 Lansdown Industrial Estate,

Gloucester Road, Cheltenham, GL51 8PL   Tel: 01242 584984

SNOWSHILL VILLAGE

F irst of all I must write a little bit about the village of Snowshill, where I have lived all my life. To me Snowshill is the prettiest and most unspoiled village in the Cotswolds and I have never ever wanted to live anywhere else and if I could have my life over again, I wouldn't want it to change much, except perhaps to have a little more money and not quite so much hard work.

I consider myself very lucky to have lived in the village where I have so many friends and family. It must be awful living on your own in a town, where you hardly know your neighbours. One of the times when you appreciate Snowshill the most is when you have had a day in town shopping; there everyone seems to look worried and in a hurry but you come home to peace and quiet and people you know.

Snowshill has a population of around 140 residents and although there are almost twice as many houses today, the population in my boyhood was not much different. Years ago, practically all the villagers were land workers and families would average around five or six per house, whereas today there are about 2 to 2.5 per house, as a lot of the younger people have married and left the village to find better employment.

Quite a number of old cottages have been bought and modernised by retired people from towns. Old stone barns and sheds have also been converted into houses and quite a few are being let for holiday cottages, which I think is a shame, but I suppose you have to accept things like that, as it's happening all over the country now. I suppose you can't blame people for wanting to spend a holiday in our lovely village.

Until the last year or two all the houses and buildings were built with locally quarried stone and slates, but old Cotswold stone and slates are becoming increasingly difficult to find these days. So they have begun using reconstructed stone and slates which after a year or two blend in well with the rest of the village and you can hardly tell the difference, so the village itself hasn't changed much, except that it's expanded a bit.

But village life certainly has. The locals are well outnumbered but they still have quite a say in the running of the village. Whereas years ago the village was overrun with children, nowadays there are very few young people; the majority are middle-aged and retired people and so life is entirely different. Years ago with only push-bikes for transport, compared with the motor car today, people had to rely on one another and so everyone was more friendly. We have had some very nice people come to settle in the village but I think you have to be born in the country to understand it properly.

Snowshill around about the turn of the century

PARENTS

This life story or "diary" is being written more or less as I talk, so it will be simple (like me) and without any big words and the wording and spelling will probably be a bit difficult to understand, but that's the way I am! Anyway I hope that some of it will make a bit of sense.

Now I will try and write my life story right from my birth. I was three weeks old when my parents moved to Snowshill in 1914, although I was born at Snowshill Hill, which is two miles out of Snowshill, but still in the parish, so I am a local born and bred.

My father when working as a groom at Snowshill Hill

At that time my father was employed as groom at Snowshill Hill. My grandfather on my father's side came from Norfolk where he had been a small farmer, but like most farmers in those days, had a job to scratch a living, so he packed up and moved to Willersey, where my father was born. My father was one of a family of nine, although three died with diabetes in their early twenties (just before insulin). They lived at Willersey for a few years, where my grandfather tried to work a small holding, without success. So they moved up to Snowshill where my grandfather took a job on a farm at Brockhampton.

When my father left school, he took a job as a groom and travelled around a lot, breaking in and training polo ponies, at which I'm told he was very skilled. During his travelling around he met my mother, who lived in a village called Longworth in Berkshire. She came from a family of thirteen and although she was about the middle one, she outlived them all, living to the great old age of ninety-five and a half, so the Snowshill air must have suited her.

My parents were married at Longworth in 1911 and came to live at Snowshill Hill in 1912 and from there they moved to Snowshill in 1914, so neither of them were locals. I think my mother had rather a hard time when she first came to live in the village, as nearly all the villagers were married to local people. She was treated like a foreigner, but being a very strong willed person, she soon sorted things out and after a few years in the village had quite a say in village affairs.

My mother had four children all in the space of four years and four months. I was certainly the smallest of the litter and seemed to have more ailments than the rest.

My older brother Jack is as fit as anyone in the village, he certainly works as hard. My younger brother Eric was always the wild one of the family. He was like my dad, went from

job to job; he finally decided to emigrate to Canada and has
lived there for about 40 years now. He has been home twice
in that time, but has always been keen to go back. He has
settled down at last and loves the life out there. My sister
Norah has lived in the little village of Fifield in Oxfordshire
for the past 45 years. But Jack, like me, has lived in
Snowshill all his life.

My mother and father's Wedding group.

CHILDHOOD MEMORIES

There are three things that seem to stick in my memory as a child. The earliest one that stands out the most was when I was barely two years old. It was of my father bending over me, with a peaked cap, shiny buttons and a big moustache. He had just come home on leave from the army, where he served in the Coldstream Guards for about 18 months until he was invalided out with ear trouble. The sight of what I thought was a complete stranger scared me to death and I can still see his face as if it was yesterday.

The second thing that I remember most is me lying on our sofa and one of my playmates brought me a young bird in a nest. I think it was a blackbird. I had just come round after falling on the back of my head and had been concussed for a couple of days. I would think that I was about three years old then.

The next thing that still stands out in my mind is my mother holding me up to watch my dad go into a yard full of horses, swinging a rope round like a cowboy and lassoing one of them with help from other men. They saddled and bridled it and Dad got on its back and of course it reared up and bucked all round the yard and I was taken away screaming my head off. That is the only thing I remember about my dad working with horses, because soon after that he finished with horses and settled down in the village, working on the building for a while and later becoming a gardener, a job he did for 37 years.

POOR BUT HAPPY

"Poor but happy."—I think that is a very good description of my early village life. When I say "poor" I mean very little money, but in spite of that everyone was happy. Wages those days were 30 shillings a week or £1.50 in today's money. That meant working over 50 hours a week and out of that most families had to pay about three shillings (or 15p) a week rent which brought it down to around 27 shillings. Most of the villagers worked on the land, a few were gardeners and carpenters, also quarry workers and grooms, but the basic wage was about the same. Most of the men could use a scythe and cut grass or corn as short as a lawn-mower does today. I was never much good with a scythe but it used to fascinate me to watch the older men, swinging a scythe. It seemed effortless and they would go on all day, stopping occasionally for a drink of either home-made wine or cider.

Everyone was living in the same type of cottages and earning near enough the same wage. So there was no class distinction, that's why everyone seemed so happy and helped one another.

There were two families of "gentry" as we called them, living in the village and about three farmers who employed quite a number of men. But the farmers themselves were having a hard time and most of them went bankrupt in the end.

It was only during and after the 1939-45 war that farming really started to flourish, as a "War Agricultural Committee" was formed and although farmers were advised on what crops to plant they were also subsidised on most things so they really couldn't go wrong. Money was very tight in my younger days, but everyone had allotments and so they had plenty of vegetables. Practically everyone kept pigs and poultry, also tame rabbits for food; there were also plenty of wild rabbits and the occasional pheasant. So really we lived more or less off the land.

I could shoot and snare a rabbit before I left school and in fact sometimes had to go round my dad's snares before going to school. It all sounds a bit bloodthirsty today, but we did it for food not pleasure. It was the way we were brought up those days. Pork, rabbit, bacon, eggs and potatoes were probably our main diet. Nearly all the cottages had a pig-sty and fowl pen at the top of the garden, where they kept one or two pigs and from the end of October until March, pigs were being killed every week and nothing was ever wasted.

PIG KILLING

S aturday afternoons were usually the pig killing day and they were very gruesome affairs. A few were killed on the village green, but a lot were killed in back gardens. Most of the village would turn out, and all the kids had the time of their lives. The pig killers were mostly local, and my Uncle 'Joe Russell' was a village pig killer. They were always a bit tipsy when they started as they were drinking home-made wine most of the day, so quite a few mistakes were made.

They would set up the pig killing bench on level ground then go into the sty and catch the pig by putting rope into its mouth and pulling it tight. The pig would be dragged out of the sty squealing and struggling, then 2 or 3 of the men would pull it onto the bench and hold it firm. Another rope was tied onto one of the front legs, then a couple of boys were allowed to hang on the rope to keep it clear of its throat. The pig killer had to feel for the right place to stick the knife in. Sometimes they hit the jugular vein first time, but quite often they had two or three attempts (through too much to drink). One of us boys was allowed to hold a bucket to catch the blood, which was usually put around the rose trees. I can remember one pig that was killed on the green, that struggled off the bench after it had been stuck and ran quite a way, being chased by half the village, until it dropped down dead.

In later years, just before the war, a man called 'Arthur Tidmarch' did a bit of pig killing. He was very slow and deliberate, but would make an excellent job of it. I remember him turning up to kill one of my dad's pigs with what they called a humane killer. It was like a large pistol and when it was fired it was supposed to drive a spike into the pig's brain. I remember him saying "It won't feel a thing.", but each time he fired the gun it just glanced off the pig's skull, so in the end he stunned it and stuck it. Either the pig's skull was extra thick or the gun was no good, but most pig killers were using them with great success at that time. In fact you were not allowed to kill a pig without stunning it first, and not long after that pigs had to be sent to the butchers to be killed and dressed. When all the innards had been taken out, the pig was then propped up against a wall in the wash-house or shed so that it would set firm, ready to be cut up on Sunday morning. The hams and sides of bacon were then placed in salting trays in a cool shed or cellar and salt rubbed into them for a week or two. Then they were placed on racks on the ceilings of the cottages or the bacon sometimes hung on the wall, like a picture, and from there it was cut and used as you wanted it. I don't know why, but the bacon today is tasteless compared with our home-cured.

The pigs didn't cost too much to feed as practically everyone grew half a ton or more of potatoes and the small and deformed ones and all the household scraps and peelings were boiled up and put into a "hog tub" as we called it, which was a large barrel sawn in half. This, with a bowl of barley meal a day was all it cost.

When someone had just killed a pig, they would save all their scraps and slops and give them to someone who was feeding one. So when a pig was killed, small joints and liver etc. were shared out with other families and in that way everyone had fresh meat or "fry" as we called it, all winter, and the bacon lasted all summer. The pigs played an important part in our lives and so with everyone keeping a few hens we were able to live reasonably well. Plenty of vegetables were also grown, as most families had allotments as well as their gardens and all the family helped with the gardening and harvesting the potatoes and other vegetables.

LIVING CONDITIONS

"Very primitive". That's a good way to describe our living conditions, as practically all the cottages were in very poor condition and quite a few were condemned as unfit to live in as the slates were falling off and the wet came through the roof. The landlords didn't seem to care and so you had to do a lot of repair work yourselves.

Most of the cottages had one small living room and a small dark little place, which we called the pantry. It was used for a number of things, washing up etc.; quite a few hadn't even got a window and in the winter you did most of the job by candlelight. The coal hole as we called it was usually under the stairs and when you could afford to buy coal it was carted through the front door and dumped under the stairs, making quite a dust. There were two small bedrooms to most of the houses although one or two of the better houses had three. The rooms always seemed warm, I suppose being so small and having such large families living in them helped a lot. All the cottages had the same type of fireplace, which was raised about a foot off the ground, with a large oven on one side, and what we called a hob on the other. You could stand the kettle on the hob and it would be always just on the boil.

Most villagers had a large iron cooking pot, which hung over the open fire on a chain and hook. It looked a bit like the pots that cannibals boil people in. There were and still are plenty of woods around Snowshill, so when we couldn't afford to buy coal, our job was to go and get what we called

The cottages where we lived before they were modernised. My sister Norah standing outside with my dog Topsy.

'shoulder sticks'; which were thick boughs of wood, also kindling wood which was tied up and called a burden of wood. When we had got it home, we sawed up the large pieces and chopped a big box of wood up for kindling. That was one of our Saturday morning jobs. After that we were allowed to go out to play.

Most of the houses had a large outhouse, which we called a brewhouse. This was usually shared between two to four families. It was really a wash-house with a large copper, but I suppose it got the name brewhouse because there was so much home-made wine brewed in it and there were always one or two large half barrels of wine fermenting in there. Sometimes the odd mouse or rat got drowned in it, but it was fished out and the wine drunk just the same.

Wine was made out of almost anything and I know my mother used to make about six gallons a fortnight. News soon got round when someone had a 'drop of good' and you always had plenty of visitors. Sunday morning was the main wine drinking time. There was always a gang at our house when we had some on tap and they would stand round the barrel and draw it in quart jugs. I have known them to drink it while it was still fermenting.

Snowshill was quite famous for its home-made wine and when a 'whist drive' and dance or a social evening was held in the village, there was someone knocking at your door all hours of the night. Quite a lot came from neighbouring villages, including Broadway, to sample our home-made. It was usually a very friendly atmosphere, but sometimes there were a few fights, when some of the younger ones had a drop too much, but they were good clean fights 'with fists', not like today when they kick and stab you, and in the morning they were usually best of friends.

There was a large copper in the brewhouse which was used for the week's washing and this was shared with three or four families, although a few houses had their own. So each family had a certain day for the use of it. There were sometimes a few arguments because someone had left it dirty or untidy but again that was part of village life.

Water was quite a problem as there were just two taps, one at each end of the village, from which water was being endlessly carted, although about three or four had their own wells. Sunday night was usually the main water carrying night. We would probably carry about twenty buckets between us and fill up tin baths and tubs, ready for washing etc. Our family was lucky because the nearest tap was only about thirty yards away, whereas some families had to carry it 200 yards or more, which made water very precious.

The same water was used for quite a number of things, like washing up the pots and pans etc., and with only a candle for light during the winter months and a bowl to wash up in, you can guess that some of it was none too clean when it was finished. I know the water used to look more like soup when you had finished, as of course there were no sinks in those days. Bath night was nearly always on a Saturday in a tin bath in front of the fire and with sometimes about six children being bathed. The last one in was unlucky as we all used the same water, which was topped up occasionally with a kettle of boiling water. As we got older we either had a bath in the small pantry, if there was room, or in the brewhouse, with a sheet hung over the window.

The only lighting was from an oil lamp nearly always in the centre of the table, the rest of the house lit with candles. Sometimes you had a torch, if you could afford the batteries. Torches were mainly used for going to the lavatory which was nearly always at the top end of the garden, sometimes as far away as 30 yards. I suppose they had to be because of the smell. A lot of them were what we called vault lavatories, which meant that there was a bricked-in pit which was only cleaned out about twice a year. This was done by lifting a slab outside and scooping it out with a kind of ladle on a long pole and tipping it into a wheelbarrow, then wheeling it to the top of the garden and burying it. Our neighbour always emptied his into his celery trench and grew the best celery in the village, but I'm afraid I didn't fancy any.

The vaults were usually shared between two or three families and there was always someone trying to miss a turn (you couldn't blame them really). I know you had to be very careful where you walked for the next few days after that episode. A few of the houses had large buckets which were much better, but they were apt to let them get over full, which often resulted in a shoe full, which wasn't very pleasant. The toilet rolls those days were the "Daily Mail", "Evesham Journal" and the "Birmingham Gazette" which were cut up in squares and a piece of string threaded through the middle and hung on the wall.

Some of the vaults were two-seaters, with one hole smaller than the other, which I believe was meant for a child, although I don't remember ever sitting next to anyone. So after all that no wonder everyone had a chamber pot or 'Jerry' as we called it under the bed.

Our hot water bottle was a builder's brick heated in the oven and wrapped in a piece of blanket and that was just to warm the bed if we had a cold or were ill but most families had to share beds so we kept one another warm.

This picture shows the condition of the roofs round about 1930. Dad is sitting on the steps reading the Daily Mail and Topsy is asleep. The door on the extreme right used to be Turner's shop, you can see the sign over the door. On the left are two locals; Eric Russell and Tommy Holmes.

My brother Eric, sister Norah and me outside the old 'Brewhouse'. I'm on the right aged about seventeen.

SCHOOL LIFE

S nowshill had its own little village school which was always full. It stands in the centre of the village and its outward appearance hasn't changed at all. The school bell is still on top of the roof. But inside it is a little different because it is now used as a village hall. A new kitchen and toilets have been built at the back and although it isn't used much, it is all in very good condition and it's nice to think that something of old Snowshill is still there.

It was closed as a proper school in 1926, although it was open for two or three years after that for the under tens. We then had to walk either to Stanton or Broadway. Most of us chose Broadway although it was three and a half miles compared with two miles to Stanton.

There was a lot of ill feeling in the village when the school was closed. I believe the reason they gave was that they couldn't get a teacher to stay. That was probably true as they had about four teachers in my short time there. It was a Church of England School and so the vicar (who was vicar of Stanton and Snowshill) had a big say in the school affairs and we were told that we all had to go to Stanton school which was a C of E school. But most of our parents thought differently and decided to send us to Broadway, which was a council school. I believe that caused more ill feeling, although two or three of the 'yes-men's' families went to Stanton.

I don't remember much of my first few years at school, except that the school was always full and we were very happy. Some of us were only three or four years old when we started, but we were only a few yards from home and our mothers would keep an eye on us at playtimes etc. There were two teachers. The infant teacher was a village person and about the only thing she taught us was religion and good manners, something the children don't seem to be taught today.

The school was very cold in the winter, as it had a very high ceiling and the only heating was an open fire, but we never saw much of the fire as the teacher's desk was right in front of it and the teacher sat with her back to it, so she was the only person who was warm.

On very cold mornings, the desks were moved into the middle of the room and we all marched round and round singing "here we go round the mulberry bush" while the teacher played the piano. After about half an hour of that, we were warm enough to do our lessons.

There was no running water and the toilets were two buckets, which were emptied by two of the bigger boys, in holes dug in a plot of land attached to the playground. We named the toilets 'Dock Leaf Dell' because there was always a shortage of newspaper so a handful of dock-leaves were used, as there were always plenty growing in the playground.

The school was closed when I was 12 years old, so I only had two years at Broadway school, as we left when we were 14. About 40 children attended the school at that time. A few came from neighbouring farms and they would come into school with their boots plastered with mud, after taking short cuts across ploughed fields.

Going to Broadway school was quite a big thing for us, almost like going to college. What with proper class rooms, central heating, water taps, and electric lights, it was quite a change from our primitive little school.

There were no school buses or meals those days. We started off about 8.00 a.m. to walk the three and a half miles, taking a few sandwiches, which we had often eaten before we arrived at the school and got home about 4.30 to 5.00, which made it quite a long day. We did occasionally get a lift home on an old lorry, but there was hardly any traffic on the roads those days.

The first bicycle we had was an old ladies back-pedalling brake, which was shared by the three of us, as my elder brother Jack had left school by then. I think it cost my dad about 5/- or 25p. We all learned to ride on it. I think that I was about thirteen and a half years old and the last few months I was at school we took it in turns to ride it to school. One of us would ride it to the bottom of Snowshill hill, then leave it in the hedge for one of the others, who were walking behind to ride on until they caught you up. There were always arguments about the last one to ride it coming home, as that was the one who had to push it most of the way up Snowshill hill.

There were five teachers at Broadway - Headmaster, deputy master and three female teachers. I think that if I had had a bit longer there, I would probably have made a better job of this writing, but having just got settled in, it was time for me to leave.

We were called all sorts of names when we first started school. The one that stuck with us was the Snowshill-Swede-Gnawers, because at that time fields of swedes were grown on the hill for fodder for the sheep and I think they had the idea that we lived on them. We did cook quite a few.

CHRISTMAS IN THE '20's

T he four events we looked forward to most during my childhood were Christmas, Snowshill Wake, St. Barnabas and Bonfire Night.

Christmas was probably the one we liked the most and I know we believed in Father Christmas when we were seven or eight years old, but children today see so many Father Christmases on TV and in stores that they get a bit confused.

Christmas was a very happy time for us and although there was very little money about, we always had our stockings filled with small things. Some of them we had every year, like an orange, apple, handful of nuts, transfers and always a sugar mouse or pig with a string tail.

But we did have one major present, something like a torch or box of paints and the girls had a doll or doll's house, sometimes homemade. Not like today when children have presents like bicycles and radios, but I think we appreciated our little presents much more. After the excitement of opening our presents there was Christmas dinner to look forward to; not many families had a turkey; but there were plenty of home fed cockerels and pork so we had quite a feast. Nearly all the families made their own Christmas cakes and puddings. We always gorged ourselves on the puddings as most mothers put three penny bits (which were little silver coins) in the puddings and of course we were allowed to keep them if we were lucky enough to find one.

There was no TV or radio then, so after tea we made our own amusements, like playing games and having a sing-song, usually carols, especially if someone had a piano. We usually had our band, which was a melodian, which my mother played, a mouth-organ and a biscuit tin for drums. After we had gone to bed the grown-ups sometimes played cards and drank homemade wine. Nearly all the villagers turned out for Church Service, not like today when the congregation is about twelve.

SNOWSHILL MUMMERS

A nother thing that everyone looked forward to was the 'Snowshill Mummers Play,' which was performed by our fathers. There were seven of them in the play and they usually started a few days before Christmas travelling to all the neighbouring villages and large houses, either on foot or bicycle. They came home each night tired, drunk and happy and with a little more money, because after each performance they would go round with a frying pan collecting money. So after about a week they would have quite a bit of pocket money to share out.

The play was a kind of rhyming play, which didn't seem to make a lot of sense. It started off with Father Christmas walking into the room and saying his piece, at the same time moving the chairs back to make room for the performance. Then in walks 'King George' and challenges 'Bold Slasher' to a fight, in which 'King George' is killed.

The doctor is called in and with the help of his assistant, they bring 'King George' back to life. 'Beelsebub' then walks in and threatens them all with his club, if they don't behave themselves. It ends with 'Fiddler Wit' walking in with his fiddle and suggesting a song. They end the play singing "Darkies Lead a Happy Life" accompanied by "Fiddler Wit." During the song 'Beelsebub' goes round the room collecting money in his frying pan. That's a rough idea of the play.

But the funniest part was when one or two of them forgot their lines and made the rest up, or one of them fell over through having too much to drink. But they were in great demand and were asked to play in such places as the Lygon Arms and Stanway House.

My dad played the part of 'Fiddler Wit' and had to black his face as of course they all wore disguises and different costumes. There were times when Dad came down stairs in the morning with half of his face still black due to tiredness, poor lighting and a drop too much to drink. But they were happy times. It's a pity that old country traditions like that have to die out.

I think the last time the 'Mummers' was performed at Snowshill was 20 years ago at Snowshill Manor. I was working at the Manor at the time and we were holding a village Christmas party there and I thought it would be nice to do the Mummers Play, as there were two of the original mummers still living. Also I knew the play off by heart, so we had a few copies typed out and got four more locals to volunteer. We collected costumes, had one or two rehearsals and did the play.

It wasn't a great success as a lot of them forgot their lines, but there were a lot of new people in the village then and they thought it was good. I still have one or two copies of the play, so perhaps in years to come, someone will want to revive it.

My dad told me how the Snowshill Mummers were first formed; he said that just after the 1914-18 war, himself, Jerry Diston and Walt Meadows walked to Blockley one night and met a man in one of the pubs, and after buying him two or three drinks, he gave them the script. There was some talk at the time that he had stolen it from Campden, as I believe the 'Campden Mummers' had been doing the play long before the 1914 war. I don't know if that is true but we always called it the "Snowshill Mummers".

They did the play from about 1919 until the mid 30's and then it ended. Dad said they were stopped by the local police

24

one night and asked if they were doing it for a charity. When they said they were doing it for a bit of pocket money for themselves they were told that it was illegal for self gain, that frightened them a bit so they ended it. It seemed such a shame as they were nearly all men who had come home from the war with no jobs, no money and large families to support, and were glad of a little extra money.

This is a picture of the second generation of the Snowshill Mummers and was performed by special invitation at a party at Stanway House in 1936, for what was probably one of the last times.

Left to Right - W.Turner (Bold Slasher), B.Smith (The Doctor), R.Turner (King George), J.Smith (Beelseebub), E.Meadows (Father Christmas), W.Meadows (John Finney) and W.Smith (Fiddler Wit).

SNOWSHILL WAKE

The next big event we looked forward to was Snowshill Wake and for a small village I'm told it was one of the largest and most popular Wakes around this district. People walked miles to go to Snowshill Wake. I can only remember the last two or three and they were getting smaller each year, but our parents had told us about all the stalls etc. taking up every little space in the village and of hundreds of people from all the neighbouring villages. The stalls were put up anywhere on the roads or in front of houses and horses and donkeys wandered about the village grazing. Of course most of the vehicles were horse-drawn then so there was no traffic problem.

There was a large marquee (or boozing tent as it was called), on the village green, which was always full. I can remember the last two "boozing tents," one in the village and the last one just out of the village at the top of Snowshill hill

in a field called the Home Ground, which at that time was the village cricket ground. It is now used as a National Trust Car Park. How times change.

We would start saving our pennies weeks before the Wake and would have something like two shillings or 10p on the day. But those shillings seemed to go a long way as we had rides on most of the things and went home loaded with coconuts, sticks of rock and small items we had won.

I was about 13 years old when the last small Wake was held at Snowshill. It was nearly all owned and run by Frank Birch and his large family. There was trouble erecting the Round Abouts or Jinny Horses as they were called then, so part of the churchyard wall had to be taken down to allow them to go round. They got us children to help remove and stack the stone and promised us a free ride, but on the night they didn't keep their promise until my dad and a few of his friends went down and threatened them. There was almost a fight, but we all got our free ride.

The Jinny Horses were pulled by a pony which was harnessed to a frame and it spent all night trotting round and round. The poor thing was kept going by little Willy Birch with a long-handled pony trap whip. In the centre was a barrel-organ at which Ben, the eldest, spent all night turning a handle. It only played about three tunes so we had the same ones over and over all night.

There were the usual shooting galleries, skittles, penny in the bucket and a lot of the stalls they still have today. But two of the smaller things I haven't seen for years are squibs and elastic balls. The squibs were like a large toothpaste tube filled with water and when you squeezed it a jet of water shot out. We would creep up behind someone and squirt it down his neck. The elastic balls were made of compressed paper on a long piece of elastic, which rebounded back to you after you had thrown it. They were quite solid and you could easily knock someone's trilby hat off, then run away. Perhaps they were classed as a dangerous weapon and banned.

Most of the real old travelling people have disappeared now, which is very sad, as they were the Salt of the Earth and made lots of friends with the locals.

ST. BARNABAS DAY

S t. Barnabas day was another celebration we looked forward to, which was held on 11th June, St. Barnabas's birthday. All the village turned out for it and it started off with a free tea party held in the village school. After the tea, there was a church service. Before the service the villagers congregated outside the school, where they were headed by the Broadway Brass Band, who marched all around the village playing "Onward Christian Soldiers," followed by the Vicar and all the villagers walking in pairs and singing. There must have been well over a hundred, as by the time the band had reached the church, the last of the congregation had just started, so they were strung all around the village and the church was overflowing.

After the service it was back to the school where the band continued to play and the grown-ups danced the night away, while the children polished off the remaining cakes and sandwiches. It must be fifty years since they held the last St. Barnabas. I think there was difficulty getting the band, as the last two or three years the church organist, who also played the violin, led the people around the village, which wasn't so exciting.

As I have mentioned before, the church was always full every Sunday. I think one of the reasons for that was the choir outing. All the children wanted to be in the choir even if they couldn't sing. As the yearly outing was free and always to the seaside, it caused great excitement, as about the furthest we ever went was to Evesham.

BONFIRE NIGHT

A nother thing we all saved our pennies for was bonfire night. Weeks before the fifth of November we were out collecting wood. Gangs of us would go out with ropes. Our favourite trick was for one of us to climb a tree and tie a rope onto the end of a branch, then about six of us would tug on the rope until the branch either snapped or split. We would get a good pile of branches, rope them together and drag them to the village green, where we spent hours stacking them and then restacking again.

We started collecting fireworks as soon as they came in the shops and every time we had a penny or a half-penny we would buy a couple of fireworks. It was always a competition to see who could get the largest collection. A time was always fixed for lighting the bonfire, which was done by the men. After the fireworks and the fire had burned out, us kids would roast potatoes in the ashes and someone usually cooked sausages. With bread, cheese and pickles, beer, cider and pop from the pub we made quite a night of it.

POCKET MONEY

We were always short of money and would do anything to earn a few pence. We tried a number of schemes. I think the one that paid the best was snaring rabbits and also selling the skins. We would sell the odd rabbit or two and collect as many skins as we could, as each month a Rag and Bone man came round the village shouting "rags, bones and rabbit skins." We sometimes had quite a collection of skins, for which we got about one penny each.

Another thing we tried was mole catching. Three of us boys had about five traps between us. We would set the traps at weekends and go round them before we went to school, sometimes in the dark as it was a winter job. We would catch about two dozen moles during the winter months. They were skinned and the skins tacked out on a board until they were dry, then packed and posted to a firm in London. We were watching for the postman every morning as we never knew how much money we were going to get for them. They were graded and ours were usually a bit blotchy through inexperience, so we had rather low grades. I think the most money we had for a winter's work was ten shillings between the three of us.

Another thing we did during the spring and summer months was to sell bunches of primroses, snowdrops and wild daffodils. To collect the daffs we either cycled or walked to Stanway where they were growing wild on private land, but by paying one shilling, or sixpence for children, you could pick as many as you could carry. We used to go home loaded, then bunch them up and try to sell them round the village. We also tried selling them out on the road. We would spend hours waiting for the odd car or cyclist to come along. Sometimes we were lucky and sold quite a few bunches to them, but another day nothing, so it wasn't a very profitable job.

All the roads around Snowshill had gates across the roads which separated each field as all the farm animals grazed all over the roads in those days. So anyone in a car or pony and trap had to keep getting out to open and shut them. Of course if there was no stock in the fields the gates were propped open. So one of the things we did in our holiday was to close the gate if it was propped open, then keep out of sight until we saw a car coming, then just before the car got to the gate one of us would run to open it. We sometimes got as much as sixpence for that. I suppose the few people who owned cars at that time were quite wealthy, but sometimes the same car came back the other way and we were told off, as they knew there was no stock in the fields.

We were always sure of sixpence every Saturday as Captain Scott who owned the land from Buckland to Snowshill used to ride his horse around the estate every Saturday morning. We were always looking out for him and could see him on his grey horse a mile away. So we used to take it in turns to run to the nearest gate which was about a quarter of a mile away, and close it if it was propped open, then hide until he got close, then run and open it. He must have known, but he always had his sixpence ready and would throw it to you with the words "can you play cricket?" for you to catch.

CRICKET AND THE MILVAINS

Two of the nicest people who ever lived in Snowshill were Major and Mrs. Milvain. They seemed to devote most of their life to the welfare of the village. I will mention just a few of the things they did. They formed a boys cricket club, taught us boxing and cooking, ran a library from their house every Sunday afternoon and found us jobs in our summer holidays.

Snowshill had always been famous for its cricket and we could hold our own with teams from Broadway, Stanway and Stanton, thanks to the boys club which was formed by the Milvains who lived at Greenclose. They spent nearly every Saturday afternoon in the summer taking us and helping with the matches. Mrs. Milvain would do the scoring and the Major would umpire. He also taught us quite a bit about cricket, as he had been quite good in his younger days.

We were also given a free tea at Greenclose every home match and the Major even mowed our pitch, which was in a little field just outside the village. The 17th Wimbledon Scouts came to Snowshill every summer for about a month, camping on Milvain's land and we had about four fixtures with them each year, which were quite enjoyable. I think they came from quite a posh school, but we looked forward to them coming, as they would invite us down to supper and a sing-song at their camp and before they left they would put on a show for the village at the village hall.

For the away matches, the Milvains also provided transport, which consisted of an old Buick car, pony and trap and a little shetland pony called Bonnie which I, being the smallest, was allowed to ride. I think I enjoyed that as much as the cricket.

I'm afraid we weren't the best dressed team in the Cotswolds as we couldn't afford to buy cricket flannels and such, but a few of us managed to get hold of the odd pair of boots or shirts from local rummage sales. So for the first season or two we were rather a motley crew with the odd one or two wearing white boots and trousers, but after a year or two we had quite a respectable looking team.

The first Snowshill Boy's Cricket Team, (I was not quite old enough to play).

Left to right: Les Diston, Jim Diston, Reg Turner, Reg Diston, Max Hardiman, Stan Aston, Jack Hodge, Max Jacques, Frank Warren, Bernard Smith and Fred Townsend.

If you did anything outstanding in a match, Major Milvain would present you with a green cricket cap with SBCC (Snowshill Boys Cricket Club) on the front. It was everyone's ambition to win one and in about three seasons we were all wearing one. I know that I was very proud when I won mine. It was at Buckland and to win it I did the "Hat Trick" (that is taking three wickets in three balls), made 17 runs and had my head cut open by a rising ball. But I soon forgot the pain when the Major said: "Well done Bobbie. You have won your cap." I still have the cap today.

They were good times and good training for the men's team, which most of us joined when we were about 14 or 15 years old.

In his younger days, Major Milvain had led a very tough life. He had been in the Yukon gold rush in Alaska and had learned to fend for himself. He had been a boxer and bare-knuckle fighter. He had survived on flour and bacon and little else. So he passed some of his skills on to us. He hired the village hall, which was an old wooden army hut from the 1914-18 war, and once a week he taught us boxing.

One or two of the lads became quite good at it, almost too good, as some of the older boys were getting too much for the Major. So he hired two professionals to teach us and exhibitions were held at the Lifford Hall, Broadway, and at Buckland and Snowshill. I was never much good as they seemed to go by your age instead of weight and as I was so small, I was usually matched against someone twice my size.

After each lesson, Major Milvain taught us how to cook, in a rough sort of way, the way he survived in Alaska. Plum Duff, Pan Cakes and Bannocks (which were mainly flour and water). Some of the boys were not much good at boxing, but they always turned up for the supper.

The Milvains had their own private library at Greenclose and Sunday afternoons it was open for an hour, for the villagers to go and choose a book. The Major was very helpful and they had a good selection of wildlife books.

As I mentioned before, we were always trying to earn pocket-money in our school holidays and that's where they helped again. We were given jobs thistle-cutting, digging docks and helping in the garden.

I have only mentioned a few of the things they did for the younger generation, but they were also good to the elderly, and it was a sad loss when Major Milvain died a bit before his time. Mrs. Milvain lived on until she was over 90 and still continued to be very helpful. You don't get people like that any more.

Me and my brother Eric, sparring

S.B. RUSSELL

S. B. Russell was another of what we call the "Gentry" of the village. In fact, the Milvains and S. B. Russell were the only ones. The rest of the village consisted of two farmers and farm labourers etc. S. B. Russell lived at Tower Close, the big house at the top end of the village. He wasn't too bad, but nothing like the Milvains. He always seemed too busy making money for himself, as he owned quite a few houses in Snowshill. He also owned the Lygon Arms at Broadway and he had just started a furniture factory at Broadway, which still goes under the name of his eldest son, Sir Gordon Russell. The hotel and factory are under new management now, as practically all the family are dead.

There was an old blacksmith's shop in Snowshill which Mr. Russell bought for a few pounds and sold to Henry Ford, the car man, who was a great friend of his and often visited Snowshill. Henry Ford had the shop dismantled brick by brick, shipping it to Dearborn, Michigan in America where it was reconstructed and still stands in the museum there. The tale was that he wanted the two Diston brothers, who were stone-masons, to go to America to rebuild it, but their wives were afraid they would get drowned and stopped them from going.

I can remember two things Mr. Russell did for Snowshill. He spent an hour in the village hall on Sundays, reading a book to us children. Books like "Uncle Tom's Cabin" and "Robinson Crusoe." Then you had to write an essay on the book and the best one won the book. I think my brother Jack won most of the books. When Mr. Russell was reading to us he always seemed to have a dew drop on the end of his nose and us kids would watch it waiting for it to fall off, but it never did, it just seemed to run backwards and forwards like a spirit-level. Some of us found that more interesting than the reading. Another thing Mr. Russell did was to invite the villagers to the hall to hear the first wireless with a speaker, because at that time some of the families had what we called "crystal sets" with earphones. They weren't very successful.

You can see the 'Old Forge' Cottage, as it is today, on the left of this painting

TOWER CLOSE

My son, Peter, did this painting of Snowshill. You can see Tower Close right at the top. I'm told it used to be two or three cottages, but Mr Russell made it into one large house. He probably called it Tower Close because it had a view of all the village. Mr. S. B. Russell and his family lived there for a number of years before the 1940-46 war. After the war it was bought by Mr Hector Smith, who lived there with his family for a long time, in fact most of the land is still farmed today by his son Donald and son-in-law Chris Byrd.

THE SNOWSHILL DOCTORS

The first doctor that I can remember was Dr. Alexander, who had a practice at Broadway. He was a proper old country doctor who did quite a lot of his rounds on horseback. If he couldn't get anyone to hold his horse, he had been known to lead it as far into the house as he could. In fact I have seen an old photo of the hindquarters of his horse just showing out of Diston's Cottage. Dr Alex and my dad got on well together as they were both horsey people at that time. Dr Alex always seemed to have plenty of time and would sit down and have a cup of tea with you. Another thing I noticed was on cold days he would always hold his overcoat inside out in front of the fire, saying it was always better to go out with a warm coat.

If you were getting over flu or some other illness, he always used to recommend a cup of Bovril, but you always felt better after having a little chat with him. I remember him coming up to Snowshill, after we had held a Boys' Boxing Tournament at The Lifford Hall, Broadway. I had boxed a draw with my opponent, which meant neither of us got a medal, but he said he thought I had won and presented me with a half-crown piece (12.5p) with a ring through it, as my medal.

He had arranged with my Dad to send me to his friend Mr Hartigan to be an apprentice at his racing stable when I left school, but I didn't go in the end, Dad was all for it, but my mother had her way and kept me at home.

The next doctor was Dr Houghton who took over the practice when Dr Alex retired. He came in the mid '30's and I believe it was his first job straight from College. He was a good doctor, young, ambitious and continually in a rush. I remember him paying my mother a visit when she was in bed with some illness. He came dashing in and threw his trilby and coat on a chair and raced upstairs. I thought that I would try his hat and coat on as he was about my size and had been parading up and down in front of my brothers and sister, when all of a sudden, he came racing back down the stairs. I just managed to get it off and fling it in the chair as he came through the door. He must have wondered what was going on, because my brothers were splitting their sides laughing.

After he had been there for a few years, a new partner called Dr Jukes came, and they both carried on until they retired a few years ago. There are 4 doctors and a nurse in the Broadway practice now; they always seem very busy and I often wonder how old Dr Alex managed single-handed.

TRADESMEN

There were quite a few tradesmen calling then, three bakers, three butchers, two or three grocers. The "Red Van," as we called it, came every week with hardware and mainly paraffin which was essential then. In fact, the Red Van still comes round today. It doesn't do much trade now. If you wanted a suit or pair of trousers, Frank Lodge, a draper from Moreton-in-Marsh, would come round and measure you and deliver, but he was rather expensive so we had a lot of our clothes either from local rummage sales or a club called the "Universal Stores," which my mother used to run. You could buy a suit then for £1.00.

A Jewish man, with a nanny-goat beard, whom we called 'Pinkus', would come round once a year with a pony and trap loaded up with boots and shoes. News would get round the village that 'Pinkus' was coming up Snowshill hill and all the women and children would be waiting for him. Most of the children were fitted out with footwear which was supposed to last until he came again in a year's time, but we were always wearing the soles out with so much walking. But most of our dads were quite good cobblers and did the soleing and heeling and some of them were quite good at stitching. I know we have had soles made from old motorcycle tyres if leather was unavailable. There were no Wellingtons when I was a boy, so most of us had really strong boots with hob-nails in to make them last.

We had one little shop in the village which was run by the Turner family. One of the descendants still lives in the house today and it is named "the Shop" although it hasn't been used as a shop for years. But it's nice to think that it's back in the family and that there are still a few Turners living in the village today. Turner is quite an old Snowshill name.

The shop sold quite a few of the essential things, but we had to either cycle or walk to Broadway to get other provisions then. Reg Burrows came from Broadway and delivered with a motor bike and box side-car. Frank Bough delivered with a horse and covered wagon like the ones you see in the films, and Doughtys came from Kineton with an old van, and a little later Charlie Jarrett came from Broadway with a van. He delivered bread at Snowshill for a great number of years and was always cheerful whatever the weather. He was one of the best.

In spite of all the pigs being killed in Snowshill there were about three or four butchers coming round. I believe they sold more in the summer months as pig killing was a winter's job and the bacon and hams were used up by the summer months. It's a funny thing, but most of the menfolk would go out to choose the Sunday joint, but my dad would never go. He always said it was a woman's job. Some of the men would spend ages trying to choose the biggest piece of meat for the least money. Balhatchets came from Blockley with a horse and cart. They are one of the very few people who still deliver meat at Snowshill today. Robinsons came from Broadway, where they still have a shop, and a little later Collins came up from Broadway and Sid Waring from Willersey. He also came round for a short time with fruit and vegetables. He was quite a character and would sell you anything.

We didn't have a milkman deliver then as one of the local farmers had a herd of milking cows. He was a Yorkshire man named Johnny Hull who came here with his son Jimmy, 75-

odd years ago. They lived at Manor Farm Cottage which is now a National Trust holiday cottage. We had to fetch our milk from the house every morning in cans or jugs. We never minded getting the milk because everyone was given a large homemade biscuit which they called a snap.

The first post office was opened when I was about four years old. It was run by another Yorkshire family called Weatherall, who were retired farmers and bought a house called Bank-Side in the village. Before that, the postman called Frank Clarke would walk up from Broadway and blow a whistle for people to come and collect their mail. Quite often he would walk 15 miles or more when he had to deliver to the outlying houses and farms. But he always found time to set rabbit snares on the way home and some mornings he would have the post-bag half full of rabbits. Three grocers would come round, the Midland Stores Broadway, J. B. Ball and Johnny Morris. They came around with horse and drays.

GAMES, AMUSEMENTS AND SWIMMING BATHS

When we were not working in our holidays, we always found something to amuse ourselves and as I have mentioned before, cricket came "top of the list." We would start playing cricket as soon as we could walk. We spent hours playing in the street with two big stones for wickets. Of course there was no traffic to interfere with you, but you had to be careful where you hit the ball and there was the occasional broken window. Also, if you hit the ball into a certain person's garden she would always keep the ball, no matter how we pleaded with her. I'm told she had a shelf full of different kinds of balls belonging to us.

The thing the older boys liked the most was when the farmers were cutting corn with the binder and horses. We had our look-outs to see who was cutting a field and when they had cut about half the field, we would go and take up positions all round the remaining corn and as it got smaller and smaller the rabbits would start running out. Of course when they came out they were a bit mesmerised and we would give chase, some times with a dog. The rabbits would quite often hide under a sheaf of corn and we would grab them. Most of the farmers would let us keep what we killed so we would often go home with two or three rabbits each. There was always someone who would give us a few pence for them.

There were swimming baths at Stanton when I was a boy and we did quite a lot of trips down to Stanton in the summer months. A lot of us learned to swim there, but I think the main reason we went was to have a good wash. It saved getting out the old tin bath. I know one lad whose mother always made him take a bar of "Sunlight Soap" with him. He would sit on the edge and lather himself all over, then lower himself in the water and swill it all off. That was his swimming lesson for the day. I'm sure his mother thought that's what the baths were for. The same baths are still used today and are quite popular.

There always seemed to be a season for everything; top-spinning was always in the autumn, followed by conkers. You could spin a top for hours on the roads then without being worried by traffic.

When it was dark at night, 'Tick Tack' was another game we played. You had a button attached to a short piece of cotton and let the button dangle in front of someone's window, securing it to the top of the window with a drawing pin. Then unwind the cotton reel for about twenty yards and hide. When you were hiding safely, you would gently tug on the cotton, so that the button went 'tick-tack' on the window. Someone would soon be looking around and when they closed the door we would start all over again. This sometimes went on for quite a time until someone laughed or was seen, but with just oil lamps for lighting, we were seldom seen.

Another game was 'Jack Shine the Light.' If we had a torch, one of us would be sent off with the torch and after about five minutes we had to try and find him. We would shout "Jack Shine the Light" and if he was a distance away, he would shine the torch, then move to another position. You could sometimes go on for a long time until you were caught. You would have a job to play that game today as there are too many lights, but then about the only light you saw was the torch.

We occasionally had a paper chase in the winter months.

We would cut newspapers up into little bits, then one or two of us would have about half an hour's start and run through all the woods and meadows around Snowshill, scattering a trickle of paper occasionally. Sometimes we were caught, but in the woods we were safe as we knew all the short cuts and hiding places. I suppose it was better than 'Fox and Hounds' and kept us out of mischief.

Nerk Meadows and Fuzzer Turner were two carters and they would plough the fields at the top end of Snowshill with their horses and ploughs and we would walk up and down the furrows for hours, just so that we could ride one of the horses back to the stables.

PETS

When we were children we had all kinds of pets. Dogs, cats, chickens, bantams, ducks, magpies, jackdaws, rabbits, squirrels, ferrets and pigs. Nearly every family had a dog or two. We always had dogs and like a lot more families, we used them for rabbiting and rat catching. There was a plague of rats and mice; all the corn ricks around the village were proper breeding grounds for them. When they threshed a rick of corn, as many as 100 rats were killed and hundreds of mice.

They usually stayed in the rick until the last layer or two of sheaves were lifted. Then they would start running all ways. That's where the dogs came in handy. Not many got away as the farmers usually ran some wire netting around the rick so we had a better chance of killing them.

Most dogs were quite good at catching or helping us to catch rabbits. We had a crossbred collie-retriever called Topsy. She was a good old bitch and had a lot of pups which we always found homes for. She couldn't catch rabbits running, but she was very good at finding them in hollow trees and old stone walls. She would mark the exact spot where they were and all we had to do was remove a stone or two, put our hand in and pull out a rabbit.

She was a good, faithful old dog and when she got old and was wasting away, my dad took her away to shoot her, as that was what most people did those days. I remember him saying that she turned her head and looked at him and he had to put the gun down. I think he got somebody else to do it in the end. That all sounds a bit callous, but those were primitive times and we looked on it as a kindness when anything was suffering.

There were dozens of cats in Snowshill and it seemed the more cats there were, the more mice. I think it's because they were always bringing them home and quite a few got away and found their way into the houses.

A lot of the kids had tame rabbits, but most of them ended up on the dinner table. You go to feed them one night and find one or two missing and they would be on the table the next day.

Everyone had poultry of some kind, either hens, cockerels, bantams or ducks. My dad rented a small orchard behind the houses, about a quarter of an acre. He kept about 100 assorted hens and a couple of breeding sows. He sold the eggs, but the pigs were a disaster. I know he paid someone to take about 15 porkers to Andoversford Market and they only made about five shillings each. That's about 25p in today's money and with expenses out, I think he lost on the day. He had one or two more litters, but there was no sale for them, so we killed the sows and ate them. The biggest weighed about 18 score and made some good bacon.

I remember the first time we took the sow to the boar at Seven Wells about two miles away. It is almost impossible to drive a pig anywhere if it doesn't want to go. We tried, but she wouldn't budge. Then my dad had an idea. He had an old donkey cart (no donkey) which he had bought at a sale for a few shillings. So we loaded the sow up and with dad between the shafts and us boys pushing behind, we took her all the way to Seven Wells. Of course the village turned out to have a laugh, but the next time she was in season, we let her out and she ran all the way to Seven Wells. In fact, she was there before us. How she had the sense to find the way was a mystery.

We brought a couple of piglets up on the bottle and they would follow us everywhere. One of them we had for a pet and called him 'Ghandi' after the Indian leader. I think it was because he was so skinny when we first had him. He would run in and out of the house and was very clean. He never made a mess, almost as if he was house-trained. He would play with my terrier 'Nip' just like another dog. He put on weight quickly and when he was about three score it was decided that he had to be killed. It was my pet and it upset me at the time.

Dad decided as he was so small that we would kill him and dress him ourselves. It was a long job as it was our first attempt, but we ended up with some nice joints of pork and I was allowed to sell one or two joints in the village and keep some of the money. I was sorry to see Ghandi go and wouldn't eat any of the meat at first but after a while I relented and had my share. They told me it was from another pig, but I knew different.

Me feeding my pet pigs on the frontdoor step

In the spring we would go round looking for jackdaw or magpie nests. When we found one, we would keep an eye on it until the young ones were almost fit to fly, then climb the tree and get one or two. They were easily tamed and after two or three days hand feeding they could look after themselves and eat almost anything. They were quite good pets and we had one or two magpies and jackdaws who could talk and whistle.

They were very mischievous and would take anything bright. I remember my mother losing her engagement ring when we had the orchard at the back of the house. We had a pet jackdaw at the time and he was always flying off with things out of the house and would always fly into the apple trees, which have since been grubbed up and the land split up into vegetable gardens for the cottages. About 50 years after she lost the ring, our neighbour, Stokey Diston, was digging in his garden and found a ring and my mother recognised it straight away and it was as good as ever after 50 years. The jackdaw must have taken it up into the tree and dropped it, a thing he was always doing.

SQUIRRELS AND FERRETS

As we were getting older and with only two bedrooms we were getting a bit pushed for room, but it happened that the house next door became vacant and was condemned as unfit to live in. So for a small rent, we were allowed to use it. Me and my brothers slept in the bedrooms and the downstairs room was used for a playroom and also for our pets.

We managed to catch two young brown squirrels about six weeks old and tamed them. They started eating bread and milk straight away and were gradually weaned onto cereals. They had the run of the room in daytime, but at night we put them in a cage that Dad had made. He had fixed a wheel in the cage, a kind of treadmill, and they soon learned to make it go round. But they had a habit of waking up in the middle of the night and having a go on it. They made quite a din and woke us all up.

One of our friends in the village, Les Diston, found some squirrels about two or three days old and quite naked and blind. At that time they had a cat that had just lost her kittens so they put two of the squirrels on the cat and she started suckling them and brought them up. They had the run of the house and you could often see them climbing up the curtains as you walked by. They lived for quite a time. I remember one of them scalded itself in a jug of cocoa which Mrs. Diston had just made. I don't remember what happened to the other one.

A few of the villagers kept one or two ferrets. We always had a couple and when we had an hour or two to spare in the winter we would go rabbiting with the ferrets, guns, dogs and nets. Most landowners would let you on their land as rabbits were a proper pest at that time.

Boxing Day was nearly always a day rabbiting. Usually they went in gangs of four or five and took bottles of home-made wine. My dad and Walt Meadows nearly always went together with two or three of us kids to look after the dogs and ferrets. We never seemed to get many rabbits and usually lost a ferret, but nearly always found it either at night or the next day. A lot of home-made wine was drunk and they couldn't shoot very straight in the afternoon, but we enjoyed ourselves.

THE SNOWSHILL ARMS

Snowshill has always had a pub and The Snowshill Arms belonged to the Beard family for three generations. When Mr. and Mrs. Edwin Beard died, it was left to their daughter Ada to run, a job she did practically single-handed until she was 90 years old. It had been owned by the Beards, but Mr. Arkell of Donnington Breweries took it off her hands a few years before she died. Miss Ada Beard went into a nursing home when she was 90 and lived to be 93.

It was a proper old country pub as I remember it many years ago but it has been modernised and you wouldn't believe it's the same place. It is now a very popular and well-run place, but you can't compare it with the old days when the customers were nearly all village people and you hardly ever saw a woman in the pub. But some really good times were had there.

There was no bar and drink was carried up a flight of stone steps from the cellar by Miss Ada, as many as five or six pints at a time. There was just one licensed room with a fire grate about one foot off the floor and hobs on either side where the men used to warm their cider in the winter. One single-burner oil lamp provided light and old oak settles were around the walls. A kitchen table occupied the middle of the room. That was about all the furniture except for an odd bench, but it was always cozy and friendly and nearly always full, especially weekends.

I can remember the first dartboard being introduced to Snowshill. It was brought there by Freddie Dowdeswell, a newcomer to the village and also a very good player. My dad had learned to play as he had been away from Snowshill quite a lot, so the two of them used to take on all comers for two pence each (which was half a pint of cider) and they had free drinks most nights, until some of the others learned to play the hard way.

Most of the older men drank cider because it was cheaper, I suppose, but some of us younger ones drank the bottled beer, usually small 'Chelts' as we called them, because Miss Beard got them from Cheltenham; the draught beer though came from Arkells at Donnington. We preferred to drink it straight out of the bottle because the glasses always looked a bit dirty, but you couldn't blame 'Ada' for that, as all she had was a bowl to wash up in by candle-light. Even when the electric was laid on in the village, she refused to have it and still carried on with her oil lamps and candles.

Miss Beard was a lovely old lady and very independent but in the last few years she had to have a little help as she was crippled with arthritis. She was always good natured and cheerful, although eventually the place deteriorated so much that hardly anyone went in there and people were relieved when Mr. Arkell persuaded her to go into a nursing home.

The new Snowshill Arms is a very popular and well-run place. It has been run for the last few years by Hans Schad and his family and it's nice to think we have somewhere to go for a drink and a meal. We also have a skittle ally at the back of the pub and a lot of good times are had there, what with skittle matches and birthday parties. I had the honour of bowling the first skittles when it was opened as I was one of the oldest locals. Sadly not many village people go there now, which I think is a shame, as the village pub used to be the centre of village life, but then again there aren't that many 'true' locals left anyway.

Me and shepherd (Shep) Williams outside the 'Snowshill Arms'

CHANGES

Sometimes I try to compare life today with the years that I have lived in Snowshill and although life in my time was much harder, I know that I have lived through the best years of this century. Times when you could send your children out all day without fear of them being raped or murdered; you could also go out without locking your door, not that we had much for anyone to steal, and I can't remember anyone getting beaten up or mugged! Now another worry is the disease AIDS that is sweeping the world. At the rate it's spreading, it must be very worrying to a lot of people.

Snowshill is altering every year. One or two more houses have been built, others have been put up for sale. The prices are so high that it's impossible for locals to buy them. About 50 years ago you could have bought most of the cottages in the village for less money than people are asking for just one house. Apart from about three families, the few locals that are left live in one row of council houses. The rest of the village is owned mostly by retired people.

Two Dutch families and two Americans have bought cottages in the village. Quite a few cottages are only lived in for two or three weeks a year and a number are let as holiday cottages which has made social life practically nonexistent. We have one Fete every year where you meet people who have probably lived in the village for over a year whom you've never seen or spoken to before! That is the one time in the year when everyone seems friendly and happy, but after the Fete everyone seems to go back into their shell.

We did have an unusual event just before Christmas in 1987. It was the diamond wedding anniversary of two old locals, Nerk and Doris Meadows. Nerk was 88 and Doris 85, wonderful people for their age. Doris lived in Snowshill all her life and was easily the oldest local. Nerk didn't quite qualify as he was born about one and a half miles outside the village just in the Broadway district, but he was always regarded as a Snowshill man and lived most of his life at Snowshill.

They had a party at The Snowshill Arms with all their relations and friends and it was a very enjoyable evening. I believe the last diamond wedding anniversary held in Snowshill was for Doris's grandparents, Noah and Anne Daffurn.

At one time, practically all the cottages in Snowshill were rented, but now the only rented houses are the council houses and half of those are now owned by the tenants. My daughter and her family bought the council house that I live in in 1983 and it was decided that I should have my own room and stay on. So I have lived in the same house for 43 years now. Our house was built in 1947.

MY FIRST JOBS

When I left school at 14 years old, the first thing on my parents' mind was to find me a job (any job), as with four children, ranging in age from 11 to 15 and my father earning only 30 shillings (£1.50) a week, it was a bit of a struggle to survive. So you had to take the first job that came along. My brother Jack had already left school and had a job as poultry boy at Snowshill Hill which helped a bit.

I can remember my first job. It was helping threshing corn at Shenberrow. I left school on the Friday and my dad got me the job on the Saturday at two shillings (10p) a day. The hours 7 till 5. Those days most young boys were put on one of the hardest and dirtiest jobs, which was clearing away the chaff and cavins (or loose straw). The chaff came down on one side and the straw another and my job was to rake it out and cart it away in a sheet. The dust was terrible and you were on the run all day as you had to cart the chaff up steps into the tallet or granary and the straw either into the barn or cattle yard. As fast as you took one load, you had to be quick and rake out another sheet-full, otherwise it would get bunged up and you would get cussed at. I was absolutely whacked and filthy dirty when I got home.

When that job was finished my folks were on the look out for another job, but as there was no work in the village at that time, Dad took me down to Broadway to Gordon Russell's, a furniture factory that had not long been opened by S. B. Russell, who lived at Snowshill. I managed to get a job there, but was only paid 5/- (25p) per week, which was apprentices' pay. I wasn't apprenticed, but they said as I would be learning a trade (which was rush seating chairs), I would only get apprentices' pay. It was a bit of a con really, but that's how Rock Russell made his money (sweated labour).

The first few weeks were hell, as all young lads were bullied pretty badly and they played all sorts of jokes on you. Someone was having a go at you all the time. I used to cry at night and try to get out of going, but after the first few weeks I accepted it and began to fit in quite well. But I hated factory life and was always on the look out for another job.

One thing they did was send the youngest boy out to do the shopping at lunch time, they wanted two penny worth of different things which I had never heard of, and of course, the shopkeepers didn't know what I was talking about! But I think I stopped that by keeping the pennies and saying that I had lost them.

Gordon Russell's had a big furniture van which they had just bought and it used to stand just outside our workshop and at dinner times they would say to me "Would you like to go for a drive?" and sit me up in front of this van, they would show me how to start it up, and tell me to press on the accelerator and I would sit there for some time revving away while they all disappeared. I don't know what would have happened if I had been caught, as I could easily have let the brakes off.

I had been at Russell's about a year, when a vacancy for a garden boy came up at Springhill. I got the job and was paid 12 shillings (60p) a week. I gave my mother 10 shillings and had two shillings pocket money.

There were a staff of five in the garden at that time and I was what they called Bothy Boy. A bothy is the room where they had their meals. In some gardens the bothy was also used for the men to live in, but as we were all locals we just had our meals in there. One of my jobs was to keep it clean, light the fire twice a day, boil the kettle and make their cocoa, which they all drank in basins, like the three bears. I was allowed 15 minutes to do this and if it was not ready on time, I got sworn at. They were all men who had served in the 1914 war. The head gardener had been a sergeant-major and would never let you forget it. He was married and lived in the garden cottage in the middle of a big walled-in garden. I was never spoken to at meal times and had to sit and listen to their war stories every day. The same ones over and over again and for a boy of 15 it was rather boring. But when I was working it was with the head gardener, most of the time. He had been a gardener all his life and had worked for titled people in big houses around London. He was very strict but he taught me a lot in the four years I was there and I loved the work and I think that gardening was the job I always wanted to do. But I have had quite a few jobs in my lifetime.

A lot of my work was done in the greenhouses. There were five large lean-to houses, which were heated by a large coke boiler. One of my jobs was to keep it stoked up and cart all the ashes away. Another job was mixing soil for potting. I can remember the mixture now - one part loam, one part leaf mould and one half the quantity of bonfire ashes, with a few shovelfuls of silver sand and a bit of bonemeal. To sterilise it we used to put a tin bath full on top of the pot-bellied stove in the potting-shed and as soon as the insects started running about on the top, we knew it was sterilised. That mixture was every bit as good as the 'John Innes compost' that you pay all that money for today. In fact I still use the same mixture only I don't bother to sterilise it.

Left: My first job, aged fourteen at Gordon Russell's. I'm the little one!
Right: Me, the 'Bothy Boy' at Springhill Gardens.

Still a greenhouse man today!

MY FIRST BIKE

M r. Davis, the head gardener, sold me my first bike, for 10 shillings and I paid him a shilling a week and I think that was the only thing that I've ever had on instalments. It was a full- size upright bike and I had to stand on the pedals to ride it as I couldn't reach them, even with the saddle right down. I was only about seven stone then, but I grew into it in a year or two.

There was a little girl called 'Nancy Meadows' whose Grannie lived at a lodge at the entrance to Springhill Drive. (The lodge has been pulled down now, but is still referred to as 'Meadows Lodge' as a large family of Meadows were born there and lived there all their lives.) Once or twice a week 'Nancy' had to walk up to her Grannie's which was over a mile, often after walking home from 'Broadway School' to take groceries and things. (Fancy sending a 7 or 8 year old girl all that way on a lonely road today!) Anyway 'Nancy' knew that I came home from work at 5, I suppose the kid was tired out, so she would sit on the bank and wait for me to give her a ride home on the bar of my bike. It was all downhill to Snowshill so we were home in about 5 minutes. She is my neighbour now and we often have a laugh about it. If you did that today you would get some funny looks!

GETTING THE SACK (OR NEARLY)

I almost got the sack a couple of times. When Mr. Davis went on holiday, I was left in charge of the greenhouses. It was just the time when the grapes were ripening and one of the men told me that if you nipped them off from the top of the bunch no one would notice. but once I started I couldn't leave them alone and at the end of his week's holiday, some of the bunches looked like skeletons and it was pretty obvious that he would notice it and he did! I had had a real telling-off and was threatened with the sack if anything like that happened again, but just after that I did another silly thing. The peaches and nectarines were getting rather ripe and if the odd one fell off I was allowed to have it, but they weren't falling off fast enough for me, so one day I gave the wires that they were trained on a tap wih a stick and about a dozen fell off. I didn't know what to do, so I cleared off and left them. Mr. Davis came and found me. Of course I tried to make excuses, but he knew what had happened all right and that was my last warning. After that I behaved myself.

After I had been there about four years, I developed some sort of illness and was off work for almost a year. It started with a bout of flu, from which it took me ages to recover. The doctor thought it was caused by working in hothouses (the temperature in one was kept at 80 degrees) and I used to cycle two miles home after working there all day in the winter without bothering to put extra clothes on. I seemed to have one thing on top of another and was under the doctor for months, and in the end I had to leave as they had to get someone else to do my job. It must have been hard for my parents keeping me all that time, but I did get a little sick pay. I think it was about 5 shillings (25p), not much for a 19-year old.

When I began to get a bit better, I started looking round for another job and for the next 18 months I did a number of different ones. The first was helping to plant a wood on the Springhill Estate. I had about two months at that and during that winter I got jobs on Saturdays as a beater for the pheasant shoots they had on the Springhill and Stanway estates. We were paid 5 shillings a day and we also had one bottle of beer and a pack of sandwiches each, which was quite good pay in those days.

ODD JOBS

When the tree planting had finished, I had about six months working for Jim Galt at Second Brockhampton Farm. He was struggling to make a living with a few dairy cows. During the summer I helped him hoeing mangolds and swedes and carried a small field of hay. I also helped with the milking. I'm afraid it took me a long time to get the hang of it, but I didn't do too badly, as one day when he went to market, I was left to milk 17 cows on my own. It took me most of the afternoon and I hadn't quite finished when he got home about 6 o'clock. He always had a couple of 30-gallon barrels of Plum Jerkum filled every year and kept in the dairy and he used to drink it out of pint mugs. At milking time he always drew me a mug full and I used to go home half canned and had a terrible head every night.

At the beginning of autumn there wasn't much work for me to do and I found out that he was setting rabbit snares and taking the rabbits into Broadway and selling them to pay my wages. He didn't like laying me off, but he was quite relieved when I told him that I was looking for another job. As it happened my sister Norah was working at the Broadway Hotel, which had just been opened, and they wanted someone do the odd jobs inside and out. I did all sorts of jobs there from gardening to washing-up, stoking the boiler and occasionally wearing a white jacket and black trousers and taking the guests' hats and coats and carrying their cases up to their rooms (a job I hated).

I never seemed to get any tips. I used to dump their cases

and get down the stairs and quick. I was told later that the head waiter used to follow them in and hold his hand out. I never liked him anyway; he was one of the first persons I knew that wore a wig. He fell down one day and his wig fell off on Broadway Green, in front of everybody. I was there about six months when my sister got another job and the next week I had the sack. Apart from having to leave Springhill Gardens that was about the only job in which I was given my notice. I wasn't sorry as I hated the job.

STABLE WORK

My next job was a fortnight in stables at Broadway. I went there to help out as the stable-lad was away for a couple of weeks. Alf Ellis, the stud-groom, knew our family, as my younger brother Eric had worked for him when he left school. I had never done any stable work, but a lot was packed into those two weeks, mucking out, grooming and cleaning the tack. I was sent out exercising the horses in Broadway Recreation ground. I learned to ride the hard way, about two hours every morning round and round the Rec. I came off a few times and I know what it's like to be saddle-sore, but after the two weeks were up I was doing quite well and was quite confident.

I must have pleased Alf because he sent me to the Broadway Hunt Kennels for a job, which I got as they were short handed. Bill Invine, the stud-groom, didn't even ask me if I could ride. When he knew my name was Hodge he said: "That's good enough for me," as he knew all about my dad and had worked with him for a time when he was in stables. Little did he know that I had only two weeks experience!

But he was very good to me and rigged me up with stable clothes, as I was about the same size as him and I was sent out riding exercise on the roads with the rest of the string the first day I was there. They employed seven grooms at that time. You were supposed to do two horses each, but quite often you had three or four. They had over 20 horses but there was always some that were lame or had something the matter with them.

When I had been there a week or two the stud groom asked me if I would ride second horse to the first whip (who occasionally hunted with the hounds). He said that Albert Franklyn, who rode second horse to the master (Captain Bill Scott), would look after me, which he did. He taught me quite a lot about riding. He was a good horseman and had served in the Cavalry in the '14-'18 war. I was rigged out with a stable suit, bowler hat and hunting tie and off we went.

Our job was to follow along behind the hounds to the meet and keep in touch with the hunt until they were ready to change horses, which was usually after two or three hours. We were supposed to take all the short cuts and keep our horses fresh, but sometimes we did almost as many miles as the hunt, as when they blew the horn for us to change, we had to be there quick. They changed and were away in about five minutes and we were left with their tired horses to take home quietly. We nearly always had one of our own horses out and had to turn round and either wash it down or groom it and put it straight. If yours was one of the last to come in it could be 7 or 8 o'clock before you got home. Saturday always seemed the longest time and we had to be early on Sunday morning for mucking out and putting our horses straight, so we didn't have much spare time.

Long hours and poor pay was one of the snags but I loved the job and was sorry when the hunting season ended, as most of us were laid off for the summer months. The hunting season ended just before Easter that year and one of the horses that I had ridden and looked after all winter was entered for the Point-to-Point which was run at Springhill on Easter Monday. But since I had already left by then, another boy, Jim Keyte, took it up and led it round in the paddock. The horse was called Kingstreet and it won at 14/1, ridden by Major Teddy Milvain who lived at Snowshill. I would have just loved to have led him round.

The time had come for me to look for another job and I was lucky enough to drop straight into another stable job. I had just taken a part time job helping to make a fence around the garden at Rex House, Willersey, and Major and Mrs. Lane, who were keen hunting people, had just bought the house and had a stable built. They already had a groom but were looking for a stable-lad, who was willing to look after the small garden in the summer months. I told them that I had just done a season at the kennels and they gave me the job and I was there for three years. We lived on the premises as a nice little bedroom and bathroom had been built onto the saddle room (my base was still at Snowshill and I used to go home most weekends). We got our own meals, nearly always out of the frying pan. A pound of beef steak was one shilling and with a couple of eggs made a good meal, but after about a year on the same diet, we started looking for someone to cook us a midday meal and a Mrs Ingles agreed to do it. She turned out later to be my mother-in-law as I married her daughter, Mary, five years later, when she was 21. We had been courting for five years.

Photo of me when I was a stable lad for Major and Mrs. Lane at Willersey

LAND WORK DURING THE WAR YEARS

When I had been in Willersey three years Major Lane died and Mrs Lane asked me if I would look for another job as she wouldn't need two grooms. That was in 1938 and work was very scarce then. I tried all over the place and my brother Eric and I cycled all the way to Kingham near Oxford to try for a job in stables, which we agreed to take. Eric took the job and while I was hesitating about what to do Mrs Lane told me that a friend of hers named Captain Eason had just had a house built at the top of Kennel Hill which was about four miles from Snowshill, near the Stow road. She said he was looking for someone to do general estate work and odd jobs around the house.

There was about 120 acres of land, which was mainly scrub land and it needed a lot of repair work, mainly fencing. I saw the Captain and got the job on a month's trial. I remember him saying he would give me forty shillings a week, which was three shillings over the agricultural wage. He must have thought forty shillings sounded more than £2.00, but it was quite good money, as wages were just beginning to rise a bit each year. After the month was up, he seemed quite pleased with what I had done and asked me to stay on, which I did and was there for seven years. I had been there just over a year when war broke out.

When my age group came up, I registered for the Army and was expecting to be called up, but one day the Captain came to me and said that he had written to get me exempt from war service. He tried to explain to me that I would be of more use working on the land, but looking back on it he was only thinking of himself. A neighbouring farmer suggested that we work the two farms together as he already had most of the farm implements, so I was working on two farms and doing all sorts of jobs.

All the rough grassland was ploughed up for corn when the "War Agricultural Committee" was formed and farmers were told what crops to plant as the country had to be self-supporting. Drilling, threshing and harvesting corn were the main jobs. Threshing corn seemed to go on most of the winter and all the local farmers helped one another with labour and implements, and I was often working with five or six German or Italian prisoners, who could only speak one or two words of English.

There were three days that I will never forget and I have always said they were the hardest days I've ever worked. It was threshing corn for Captain Eason. Hector Smith, who had just bought a farm at Snowshill, had bought a new threshing drum; usually the old threshing machines would break down but this one went on and on. We started at 7 am and went on until 7 pm with just one and a half hours break. My job was to pitch the sheaves onto the drum; they weighed about seven pounds each. I had one German prisoner to pass them to me, but he was a bit awkward so I had to do most of it myself. It was all right doing the top half of the rick but after that it was all uphill pitching. You had to keep on non-stop, you didn't have time to wipe your nose, as the men on the drum always seemed to be waiting for more corn. We did that for three days and I had to cycle four miles home after that. I don't think I have ever been so tired in my life.

I did a number of other jobs on the farm. Drove the only old Fordson tractor occasionally but most of the work was done with horses as it was only during the war that farmers started buying machinery. I believe some of it came from America. In my spare time I did quite a bit of rabbit catching as all the farms were over-run with them (before myxomatosis). Also, they were needed for food as practically everything was rationed. I caught about 20 or 30 a week on average and the Captain used to take them to butchers. He got about 9 pence each for them, but he didn't have them all as we used to keep a few back for our own customers. I thought that was only fair as I didn't get paid any extra for catching them.

Captain Eason knew that I was engaged to be married and in 1943 he came to me one day and said that there was an empty cottage on one of the neighbouring farms (Mr. Cawley's) and if I would like it we could have it rent free. There was one condition. There were two Bramley apple trees in the garden and Mr. Cawley would like half the apples instead of any rent. I jumped at the chance and we were married on the 13th January 1943.

The house was right out in the wilds, no roads to it and everything had to be carried across two fields. I used to borrow a horse and cart to carry the heavy things, but we didn't mind that at all. Of course there was no electric and we had to carry our water from a well at the bottom of the field. I can remember two of my wedding presents. One was a load of muck for the garden and the other was two laying pullets. We had been there about 11 months and had made quite a nice little place of it, with quite a large garden. Then we had to move to Captain Eason's new lodge which he had built at the bottom of his drive, half way up Kennel hill. It was very modern, with electric and water laid on.

The reason we moved then was that Tom Swain, who also worked for Captain Eason, was living there with three small children and his wife had just left him. After a lot of thought we agreed to move there and look after Tom and the youngest boy, Ian, who was five years old. We were thinking of adopting Ian, but in the end Tom decided to put all three boys in a home at Kingham. The boys are all grown up. and married with families now, but they still keep in touch and pay me a visit now and again. We lived like that for about two years but things didn't work out. I suppose we shouldn't really have taken on a lodger and his family as we had only been married a year ourselves.

So one day I had a few words with Captain Eason and gave my notice in, but not before I had seen Mr. Everitt, who was estate manager on the Springhill estate and got myself another job with a house, only about 200 yards away at the Jockey Stables. The job was looking after cattle in the winter and general farm work. The Captain tried hard to get me to stay on and even told me that I would be left something in his will. When he died he left the man that took my job £10,000. That was a lot of money 50 years ago. So I missed out on that.

ANOTHER MOVE AND BLACK MARKET MEAT

I had only been living at the Jockey Stable for six months when my wife's mother died and her father, Albert Ingles, came to see us and begged us to move down to Willersey and live with him. We decided to keep our little bit of furniture, etc. to see how things worked out. Albert had promised me a job working with him on his two or three acres of market garden land but that didn't go at all well. So I got a job working for Jack Payne, who had a small holding at Willersey. He also did a bit of wheeling and dealing (a kind of Arthur Daly). He used to make hundreds of gallons of cider and his son "young Jack Payne" and I used to go round the local farmers and small-holders collecting windfall apples and pears and take them on a horse and dray to Ingles and Sons at Broadway.

THE CIDER DRINKERS

This photo was taken when I worked for J. Payne at Willersey. We had just finished cider making and had been celebrating with some of the real stuff.

Photo, from left to right: J. Payne (Junior), Fritz the German POW and myself with Fritz's hat on. Note the piebald dray horse and part of the cider house in the background.

We had taught Fritz a few words of English, as he was always singing German songs. "Cruising Down the River on a Sunday Afternoon" was a popular song at that time, but Fritz always got it wrong. He would sing "Cluising Down My Liver on a After Sunday Noon". I quite enjoyed working

working for Jack Payne & Son, we had a lot of fun and were allowed as much cider as we could drink.

They had an old cider press which was worked by a horse that walked round and round attached to the press and it gradually crushed the fruit and juice ran down into channels, then into a pit, where it was bucketed out into barrels and then collected by local people or taken to the big cider shed at Willersey, where it was left to ferment. Cider was very cheap then and we were allowed as much as we wanted. I preferred the perry which was made with pears and tasted more like champagne.

This all happened about two years after the war, when most things were still rationed, including meat. So Mr. Payne started doing a bit of black market work. He was always going into market and buying odd lots of pigs, sheep and poultry and I had noticed that they were disappearing and new ones replacing them. Then one day I walked round the back of the buildings and caught them in the act! They had just killed a porker and were about to cut it up. After that I was brought in on the act and given a joint each time anything was killed.

Payne had his customers for miles around and one man came all the way from Birmingham in an old car and took a load back with him. One day we had just killed a pig and cleaned it up and taken it into the shed to cool off before cutting it up, when the police sergeant turned up on his bicycle. Mr. Payne kept quite cool and took him into the cider shed, which was next door with only a thin partition in it. The old sergeant went wobbling away on his bike. I often wondered if he had his joint of pork too!

Most of my work there was market garden work and quite a lot of asparagus, broad beans, runner beans and peas were grown as well as a quantity of other vegetables. They were packed up in special crates and stacked on the roadside ready to be picked up by lorries from the markets. Some went to Birmingham and others to Coventry, Stratford and Evesham. I quite enjoyed working for the Paynes, but after 18 months I decided to look for another job.

WORKING FOR HECTOR SMITH

M r. Hector Smith had just bought a lot of land at Snowshill, also Tower Close. The farm was about 1,000 acres, including fields that he rented. He had also started growing brussel sprouts on the hills, which did well on the limey ground. My brother Jack was already working for him and told me that you could earn quite a bit more money by working piece work - if you were prepared to work. And as Mr. Smith was advertising for workers and my wife was expecting our first baby and things weren't going too well at home, I decided to see Hector Smith and got the job. He said that I should take my chances on getting one of the council houses which they had just started building at Snowshill.

I started working for Hector the first week of January, 1947 and that was the worst winter that I can remember. It started freezing in early January and snowing about the second week and it gradually got worse, with very sharp frosts day and night and heavy falls of snow every two or three days. This went on and on until about the middle of March. I used to bike or walk to Broadway, where I was supposed to be picked up by a van, but quite a few days the van was left in Broadway, while we walked as best we could up Snowshill hill. It often took us two or three hours and when we got there and helped feed the stock it was snow digging time. Of course there were no snow ploughs then and practically everyone was digging by hand. Gangs of men from the Labour Exchange were sent out to help, but as fast as they dug one road out there would be a blizzard that filled it all in again. I believe Snowshill hill was dug out three or four times and the people of Snowshill were isolated for weeks.

Gangs of people took it in turns to walk to Broadway to collect bread and groceries (there were no deep freezers in those days). Hugh Galt, who was a farmer at Kites Nest, which is at the bottom of Snowshill hill, made a sledge out of some sheets of tin and stacked crates of milk on it and pulled it up to the village with a carthorse. He did that for weeks and I think that he deserved a medal for it! I was lucky to be living at Willersey during those few months but the people at Snowshill had a very hard time. Coal was in short supply (there was no electricity then) and people were struggling through the drifts with shoulder sticks which they had managed to find in the woods. I remember Jack and Bill Smith, two brothers who lived together, had got so short of fire wood that they sawed up the line posts and then the sawing horse rather than go out and get wood.

That bad winter was followed by one of the warmest summers I can remember. I was still hoping to get the council house at Snowshill and with a little help from Hector Smith, I was told that we could have it. That was in August, 1947. I have lived there for 44 years now, after moving house five times in five years. My daughter Susan was three weeks old when we moved to Snowshill. We threw our bits and pieces on one of Hector's old farm wagons and all came up together like a load of gypsies.

I did say that I have lived at Snowshill all my life and apart from the three years in Willersey that is true. Even then I regarded Snowshill as my home and attended most things in the village. I worked for Hector Smith for seven years and during that time did a number of jobs. But the main one was sprouts - that is planting, hoeing, manuring and picking. Those jobs were done on piece-work. The average pay for picking a 20 lb net of sprouts was one shilling (5p) per net. This we did in all weathers - we even kicked the snow off them to pick. It was a back aching job and I hated it, but we did get more money. (I also got arthritis and two artificial hips which I'm sure were caused by the wear and tear on the joints).

When Mr. Smith bought the land at Snowshill, most of it was scrubland and all the stone walls were falling down and badly in need of repair. So when the sprout picking was finished, usually mid-February, my brother Jack and I had the job of pulling down and rebuilding the walls around the fields. Jack had done quite a lot of it before he went to work at Hector's, whereas I had only done a bit of gapping at Captain Eason's. But I soon got the hang of it and we were doing one chain (22 yards) a day and being paid four shillings (20p) per yard. (They get up to £20.00 per yard today). It was a very cold job, especially in February and March, which I think are two of the coldest months on the hill, as we seem to get those bitter east winds for weeks on end. We used to wear old socks and all sorts of things on our hands because our fingers would be raw after one day.

Snowshill, during the winter of 1947

BRUSSELS SPROUTS AND CRICKET

P lanting sprouts was another back-aching job. To make a bit of extra money we had to plant one acre each day, which was 4850 sprouts. I know that because the land was marked out in squares with an implement and you counted up how much you had done each day. Working among sprouts was very hard work and sometimes I wished that I'd never seen a brussels sprout. I hated the work but stuck it for nearly 14 years, just for the extra money. We would have had a job to manage on just gardener's pay especially with two children at school.

When Mr. Hector Smith moved from Offenham to live at Tower Close, Snowshill, in about 1948, he took an active part in village life. He also found work for most of the men of the village. Apart from his 1,000 acres of farm land, he started training racehorses and was very successful at it. He had about 22 horses in training at one time and employed nine or ten stable lads. He trained over 40 winners in the '47-'48 season, including five on Whit-Monday. I think the reason he had such a good start was because being a farmer he could have the best oats and hay, whereas other trainers, just starting up again after the war, were not quite so lucky. He was very good to me and let me go in the horsebox to the local meetings. Sometimes he would be waiting at the gates and get me in for nothing, or if two horses went, I would lead one in and pass as a stable lad.

Snowshill had always had a good cricket team before the war and the day that I moved to Snowshill Mr. Smith had called a meeting to try to form another team. I was quite pleased about this, as I had been very fond of cricket and had played most of my life, except for the war years. I had already had a few games for Broadway and played for Weston Subedge in '47, the year I moved back to Snowshill. The trouble at Snowshill was finding a field that was flat enough, but Mr. Smith offered us a small field near the village. The outfield had a slope on it, but after a lot of work we made quite a good wicket. We played every Saturday and Sunday and had a very good team. We could hold our own with teams like Broadway, Stanton and Campden. In fact, we could pick a team from Mr. Smith's staff alone and it was quite a needle match when we played the rest of the village. The coach was always full for away matches and it was a chance for us to take our families out for the day. We always stopped at a pub and made quite a night of it.

Snowshill C.C. about 1952 Back row, left to right: F.Turner (Umpire), Hedley Caird, Bob Diston, Henry Harrison, Jess Russell, Nancy Haines (Scorer). Middle row: Bob Hodge, Ted King, Jack Hodge, Morris Clevely, George Haines. Bottom row: Charlie Ralphs, Jack Hiscox and Bill Turner

We used to have an old wooden army hut for village functions from the 1914-18 war, but it was in a very bad state. So with the help of Mr. Smith (Chairman) and a committee we had just formed, we acquired the old school, which had been lying idle for a number of years. With a little money and certain grants we purchased it from the Church, on condition that if we parted with it the Church would have first claim. With the help of Mr. Smith's implements and material and voluntary labour it was made into quite a nice place, with running water, flush toilets and electricity. It was also used quite a lot those days by the village people. Nowadays it's hardly ever used.

Snowshill C.C. 1961 - about the last cricket team
Back row, left to right: Bob Hodge (Umpire), T. Harrison, P.Harrison,
K.Barnett, Henry Harrison, Jack Hodge, J.Russell, Molly Russell (Scorer).
Front row: Roger Hodge, K.Wheeler, John Hodge, Mick Harrison, Pete Hodge.

BACK TROUBLE AND THE SNOWSHILL MANOR

I had worked for Hector Smith for seven years when I developed back trouble, which the doctors said was a slipped disc; I was in a plaster jacket for six weeks. That seemed to be the start of my arthritis which I suffered with over 30 years. I was advised to get a lighter job, but like a fool I gave my notice in and got another job with H. J. Phipps and Sons, who were a family of market gardeners from Evesham. They had just bought Shenberrow Farm, which lies between Snowshill and Stanton. They had started growing market vegetables up on the hill and wanted someone to work there and look after the place as they only came up occasionally with their gang of workmen to pick sprouts and peas.

They told me I could still do piece-work but I would be working on my own most of the time. So I took the job, thinking that working on my own would be better than with a gang, as I could ease off a bit if I didn't feel like it. I stuck that job for another seven years. I seemed to have the seven-year itch, as my last three main jobs had each lasted seven years.

There were times when I was working at Shenberrow that I didn't see anyone for days. My bosses came up once a week to bring my wages and boxes of cartridges. I always carried a gun to keep the pigeons (which were a pest) off the crops. I also had a yard full of cattle to look after. It was always a job in frosty weather keeping the water running. It was such a poor system that it was always freezing up and I used to spend hours trying to thaw it out with bales of straw.

When I was in my mid-forties I bought myself a motor-scooter, mainly so I could go home at mid-day for an hour. It was quite handy for that, but I started riding it too late in life and was always nervous. I would only ride it to places that I knew. The Phipps owned a lot of fruit plantations around Evesham and in August and September they would fetch me down to help out for about six weeks. We picked the fruit for so much a chip or pot. At first I was rather slow but after a few days I got the hang of it and used to take my son, Pete, and my daughter, Sue, down with me during their school holidays to help. We did quite well between us and filled our dinner bags with ripe plums and pears to take home.

It was in 1963 that I decided I'd had enough of working at Shenberrow. 1963 was the second worst winter that I can remember. It only lasted about six weeks, but it was bad, deep drifts, blizzards, bitter cold winds and very sharp frosts every day. I had some very bad journeys struggling through the drifts to Shenberrow. Some days it took me two hours to get there. Then my first job was to thaw the water tanks out for the cattle, which often took two or three hours to get running, then feed them and after that walk round the crops with a gun to try to keep the thousands of pigeons off. It was black wtih pigeons in places where the wind had blown the snow off the sprouts. They were so hungry they didn't take much notice of you. After that spell of weather I decided that was enough, as one of my hips was getting quite painful.

It just happened that they needed a gardener at Snowshill Manor, as the old gardener, Victor Hands, was retiring after working there for nine years. So I saw the curator, Mr. Crosfield, and he said I could have the job. But the wages were very poor, just the minimum agricultural wage, and as I was living in a council house and paying rent, I thought we would have a job to manage. So I talked it over with my wife and as Sue had just started work and Peter was due to go to college and I was 50 years old and wouldn't be able to do market garden work much longer, I gave in my notice at Shenberrow and took the job.

That was at the end of February 1963. I started working at the manor the first week in March. That week it was very depressing and I almost packed it in. I was suffering from a bad cold, there was snow on the ground, it was foggy nearly all the week and very cold. The whole place had been neglected for years. Elder and thorn trees were growing everywhere. The lawns were like fields, most of the borders were overgrown and ducks were waddling all over the place.

I don't blame Mr. Hands for all this, as he was 73 years old then and had difficulty walking. He was unable to do much work and the National Trust trustees should have retired him years before. Instead they let the garden gradually get worse and when a garden has been neglected for two or three years you can imagine what it was like.

A Mr. Charles Wade bought the Snowshill Manor in 1919. Families of farm workers were living there at that time and what is the garden now was a farmyard. Mr. Wade started restoring the manor, which was in pretty bad shape. When that was done he started collecting antiques and anything that was old and gradually filled up the manor over the years. Espleys, a building firm from Evesham, did most of the work and my dad, who had just finished working in stables, got a job on the building.

Mr. Wade, who was a bit of an antique himself, noticed my dad working, and one day asked him if he would stay on as his gardener. In a book that Mr. Wade wrote he said that he liked his name (Hodge), also his hat, which was a cloth hat "like a keeper's." He also said Dad was very handy at his work. So Dad took the job and was there for 37 years.

Dad helped Mr. Wade lay the lawns and make borders. The builders made three terraces with Cotswold stone walls and flights of stone steps, and two pools which fed one another from natural springs. The old cattle sheds were renovated into garden outhouses. They also built a dove-cote. Mr. Wade lived in a cottage close to the manor, which is called the priest's house, as monks were supposed to have lived there at one time. He had his own workshop in the cottage and used to work all hours making garden fittings, bird cages, sundials etc. He even made a model village which he built around one of the pools; it was supposed to be a Cornish fishing village. This was built for his own pleasure and a few special friends who used to stay with him most summers. Sadly it is beyond repair now. When I started working there, I found most of the little cottages and fittings and used to put them out round the pool for the first few summers, but they gradually got damaged by the parties of children who came to visit.

My father had worked at the Manor for about 34 years when Mr. Wade decided to get married. He must have been in his late sixties by then. My dad, who had been more or less his own boss all those years, didn't like being ordered about and told what to do by a woman. So one day he lost his temper and told Mrs. Wade what he thought of her and shortly afterwards Dad got the sack, after all those years. Dad was past the normal retiring age of 65 today. But those days you worked as long as you could, as the pension was nothing.

My dad worked for local farmers and doing gardening jobs for different people until he was 73, when he died after a short illness. I remember him saying to me when the doctor told him he had only a short time to live: "What are you looking so miserable about? I know that I haven't got long but I've had a very good innings and nobody lives forever." Although he never showed it, I'm sure that having to leave the manor after all those years played on his mind and hastened his end.

When Dad left the manor Vic Hands took the job of gardener to Mr. Wade and soon after Mr. Wade handed it over to the National Trust. So it was about nine years after my father left that the job came to me. So with Dad's 37 years and my 15, we had done over 50 years between us. I like to think that between us we have planted practically all the trees and shrubs and most of the flowers that are growing there today.

ROYAL VISITS

During the years that we were there, two members of the Royal family visited the manor. Queen Mary came in Dad's time. Two remarks she made were that Mr. Wade was the biggest antique in the place and that the lawns were better than hers at Buckingham Palace, which pleased my Dad.

Princess Margaret paid a visit in my time. I will never forget that day. It was an unofficial visit and I had not been told anything about it. I began wondering what was happening when I saw some of the National Trust bigwigs and the curator and some of the helpers standing about all dressed up with their posh hats on. So I quietly got out of sight in the tool shed.

I had just peeped out and saw them all walking around the garden in pairs, when all of a sudden the curator's wife came running up the steps, all out of breath, and said: "Would you come to the top of the path as she wants to meet the gardener." I still didn't know who SHE was. I had got dirty Wellingtons on and a filthy ragged old anorak and my hands were dirty, as I had just been working in the flower borders. So I blundered out and came face to face with Princess Margaret.

I knew who she was right away but I was that flustered that I forgot to bow or call her ma'am. When she held out her hand for me to shake hands, I can remember trying to wipe the dirt off my hands on the anorak and mumbling something like: "Nobody told me you were coming." But she was laughing about it and soon put me at my ease. After complimenting me on the garden, she chatted away for quite a long time. She told me she was a keen gardener and she also knew the names of different shrubs and plants.

I think some of the toffs were a bit annoyed having to stand so long, as one of them told me after she had gone that she had more to say to me than to any of the others. It served them right really for not telling me about it. (I expect the Princess knew who did the work!)

THE MANOR GARDEN

W hen I first started working there the garden wasn't even mentioned in the Snowshill Manor notice board outside. (Just the museum). Also 11,000 was the most people that had visited the manor in one year. When I retired after 15 years it had risen to over 40,000 and quite a lot of the visitors came just to see the garden.

One of the first jobs I did was to grub up and cut down all the elder and thorn bushes that had completely covered some of the borders, and it was a job to walk down the paths in places. I must have saved the Trust hundreds of pounds by building up walls that had fallen down all around the garden. I completely built one about 25 yards long. The next job was raking the lawns which were full of moss and weeds. That was a long, hard job as there was about one acre of lawns in bits and pieces. After the lawns had been mown a few times and treated with weedkiller and fertilizer, they began to improve and when they were newly mown and edged they looked quite nice, as they were always very green. I think that was due to the underground springs that seemed to be everywhere.

There were a few old-fashioned plants still surviving in the garden, so when the beds were cleaned up, I scrounged around for different plants. I collected quite a few old cottage garden plants from friends in the village and after a year or two I had quite a collection. I had just started growing fuchsias in my greenhouse at home, so I started supplying the Manor with standard fuchsias for their eight tubs. They made enormous plants and some of them were 12 years old when I left. I still have one at home today which must be 20 years old. (Even Percy Thrower wrote about them in The Daily Mail.)

There was a large kitchen-garden which was overgrown. It hadn't had much done to it since my father worked there but with the help of Mr. Crosfield, the curator, who was a good kitchen-gardener, we gradually cleaned it and between us grew stacks of vegetables and fruit. A lot too much for own use, so we gave quite a lot away. After about a year, the garden began to take shape and people used to walk around and pass remarks about the improvement, which to me was as good as extra money. I loved the job and had a free hand, which I liked. The National Trust garden advisor would come round once a year and suggest a few different things to be done, but apart from that I was was my own boss, which was very nice.

I had been working at the manor for about two years and had just got it under control when the Trust decided to have the manor and all the outhouses re-roofed. The workmen were there for about two years or more and I was forever following behind them, cleaning up and turfing and seeding the lawns. The manor was kept open all the time they were working there which made a lot of extra work for me. The manor was re-roofed in the closed season and I was cleaning up behind them all winter. There were ruts one foot deep where they drove the dumpers down the lawn which I had to fill in and re-turf. The first winter as many as 22 men were working there, trying to get it finished before opening time. (The builders were Williams of Longborough).

THE MANOR GHOSTS

T here have always been tales that Snowshill Manor was haunted, but neither Mr. Wade or my father ever saw anything unusual. But when Mr. Wade bought the Manor and the workmen were renovating it, one of the men who was sleeping in there ran away in the night, claiming he had seen a monk. Also Dottie Dark, who cleaned the manor, was supposed to have seen something halfway up the stairs and spoke to it, thinking it was Mr. Wade. She said it had a hood on and disappeared.

I don't believe in ghosts but there was one thing that always puzzled me. It was on a dark morning in mid-winter and it had been pouring with rain all night and in the half-light I saw what I thought was a dead pigeon. When I got closer I saw that it was a doll dressed in some sort of blue material, but the funny thing was, when I picked it up, it was bone dry and all around it were puddles of water.

I knew that on the third floor of the manor there was a kind of children's nursery with very old primitive toys and such. The doll was exactly underneath the window, but the window was tightly closed; I got Mr. Crosfield, who was curator at that time, to check it.

It looked as though someone or something had opened the window and flung it out and then closed it. I could never understand what happened there and it worried me for a long time. I know that I took the doll down the garden and burnt it on my bonfire. It was an ugly little devil anyway.

The last year or two that I was at the Manor were pretty

painful as my hips were getting worse. I saw my doctor and put my name on the list for hip replacement on my right hip, which was very bad. That was in 1978 and I was told that it would be probably a two-year wait. I enquired about having it done privately and was told about two weeks. As I didn't want to lose my job and I had another two years to do before retirement, I scraped up enough money and decided to have it done.

I was in hospital eight days and started work six weeks after I came home. I worked for more than a year, but my left hip and ankles were getting quite painful. My wife used to come down and help me with the mowing, as I had difficulty walking. So in September, 1979, I decided to call it a day and took early retirement, much against my will, at age 64.

They have had two gardeners since I left and are advertising for a third. I hope it is a good one as I still worry about the garden and would hate to see it deteriorate.

Me and my prize-winning onions, when I used to do a bit of 'showing' at the local flower shows.

CONCLUSION

T he Trust was very good when I left and I was presented with a silver salver and made a life member. During the last summer I was there I received a letter from Buckingham Palace, saying I had been awarded the BEM for my work in restoring the garden. The Trust must have recommended me, but it came as a great shock, fancy a hill-billy like me getting the BEM! I think it was mainly because my father and I had worked there for over 50 years. It was presented to me on September 28, 1979, my wife's 57th birthday. Sadly, she died suddenly less than a year later on September 13, 1980.

I lived on my own for three years and did a bit of jobbing gardening, but my other hip was getting much worse and I was beginning to let the place go. So it was decided that my daughter Susan and family would sell their house and buy the council house that I was living in and move up to Snowshill to look after me.

Peter, my son, is now a full-time artist and his son, Barnaby, is ten years old. Dean, my grandson, passed out of Kingston College and lives and works in London, and Zoe, my granddaughter, is a qualified hairdresser and recently married. My wife would be proud of them all.

My sister Norah died recently after a long illness. My brother Eric and and his wife Lily paid us another visit and were here when Norah died, but had to go back to Canada the next day. I miss my sister very much, as I used to go and stay with her at odd times.

I'm getting around reasonably well but can't do much

work. I'm 77 now and beginning to feel my age.

When I started writing down these memories, the idea was that they might be something for my grandchildren and great grandchildren to read in years to come. I had given no thought to having them published until my son Peter and several other villagers suggested that I do so. It's true that even now, people don't know how we lived between the two wars.

Snowshill is becoming a village of weekend and holiday cottages; you can almost count the locals on your hands. Most of the people are very good and fit in well with village life, but the odd few are always complaining about the cars in the village. But, as I have said, we have a pretty little village, so why stop people from coming to see it?

I sometimes hobble around the village and start thinking back to the times when you could walk into anyone's house and have a glass of home-made wine and a good chat. But now it's sherry parties and coffee mornings where village affairs are discussed. I've lived here most of this century and in spite of the hard work I think the early times were the best.

I have just been reading my notes and have thought of so many more things that I could have written about. But, I hope what I have written will be helpful and settle a few arguments in years to come.

I still manage to grow a few fuschias and sell them to the visitors when the Manor's open in the warm months. People come back year after year for my plants. They seem to like a chat and when they ask questions about old times in the village, I tell them some of the stories in this little book. Later, when the fuschias bloom in their own homes, perhaps they'll remember our village and the way it was when they were young.